A Note to Parents & Teachers—

Welcome to I See Animals from Xist Publishing! These books are designed to inspire discovery and delight in the youngest readers. Each book features very simple sentences with visual cues to help beginners read their very first text.

You can help each child develop a lifetime love of reading right from the very start. Here are some ways to help a beginning reader get going:

 Read the book aloud as a first introduction

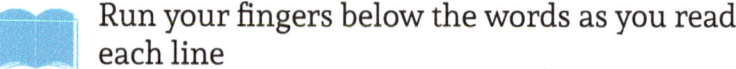 Run your fingers below the words as you read each line

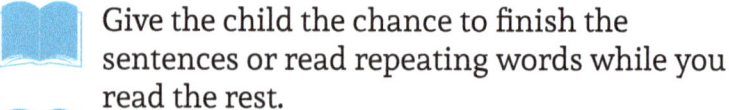 Give the child the chance to finish the sentences or read repeating words while you read the rest.

Encourage the child to read aloud every day!

Published in the United States by
Xist Publishing
www.xistpublishing.com
24200 Southwest Freeway
Suite 402-290
Rosenberg, TX 77471

eISBN: 978-1-5324-1413-8
Saddle Stitch ISBN: 978-1-5324-1484-8
Perfect Bound ISBN: 978-1-5324-4206-3
Hardcover ISBN: 978-1-5324-3403-7

© 2020 by Xist Publishing
All rights reserved
No portion of this book may be reproduced without express permission of the publisher
All images licensed from Adobe Stock
First Edition

I See Animals
Elephant

written by August Hoeft

I see an elephant.

The elephant is gray.

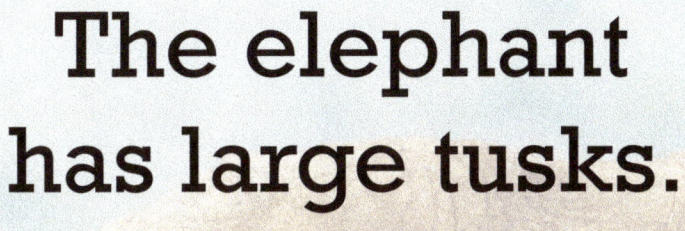
The elephant has large tusks.

The elephant eats grass.

The elephant lives in the grasslands.

I see an elephant.

Things to do next!

Write a Sentence

I see a _____.

Drawing

Make a drawing of your favorite animal.

Sharing

Talk to your classmates about your favorite picture in this book. Explain to them why you like it.

WORD LIST

an	in
eats	is
elephant	large
grass	lives
grasslands	see
gray	the
has	tusks
I	

Have you read the other I See Animals Books?

Alligator
Bear
Beaver
Butterfly
Cat
Cheetah
Chicken
Chinchilla
Chipmunk
Cow
Deer
Dog
Dolphin
Donkey
Duck
Eagle
Elephant
Elk
Ferret
Fish
Fox
Frog
Giant Panda
Giant Tortoise

Giraffe
Goat
Gorilla
Guinea Pig
Hamster
Hedgehog
Hippo
Horse
Jellyfish
Kangaroo
Kitten
Lemur
Lion
Lizard
Llama
Love Bird
Meerkat
Monkey
Moose
Mountain Lion
Mouse
Octopus
Orca
Owl

Panda
Parrot
Penguin
Pig
Polar Bear
Puppy
Rabbit
Raccoon
Rhino
Sea Lion
Sea Turtle
Shark
Sheep
Snail
Snake
Squirrel
Squirrel Monkey
Tiger
Tree Frog
Turkey
Turtle
Whale
Wolf
Zebra

www.ingramcontent.com/pod-product-compliance
Lightning Source LLC
LaVergne TN
LVHW070014090426
835508LV00048B/3411